# Beyond Passion
from nonprofit expert to organizational leader

Although the case studies presented here are derived from true stories, all characters and organizations mentioned here are disguised. Any resemblance to real names is purely coincidental.

# CONTENTS

# FOREWORD

I met Nicki Roth during my very first week as a program director for a nonprofit that she was advising. She led a retreat for the senior staff of our organization and guided my new boss on how to manage the company's meteoric growth. I had just entered the nonprofit sector after serving as an officer in the US Army for a decade. My task: reduce street homelessness in Times Square by two-thirds in three years. West Point and the military taught me a lot about leadership and getting things done, but I was utterly clueless about homelessness. I don't know whether it was seeing great potential in me or having a moment of pure pity but, as the retreat concluded, Nicki offered me additional follow-up coaching support. Less than a week in the nonprofit sector and I had a consultant with 25 years of experience to help me? I could not have been luckier.

I spent the first few months learning as much as I could as quickly as I could. I placed a tremendous amount of confidence in my boss' expertise and gleaned as much information about what I should do from each conversation with her. On one of my coaching calls with Nicki I proudly declared, "I think if I can just have one more session with my boss, I'll finally know exactly what I need to do about homelessness here in Times Square."

Next came a long pause. What Nicki said next changed the course of my life.

All of Nicki's warmth, empathy and no nonsense style came through as she delivered these words of wisdom. "I've got news for you, Becky. Your boss doesn't know what you should do. She hired *you* to figure that out."

And just like that, my understanding of myself as a leader shifted as I was gently but irrevocably pushed out of the nest and encouraged to fly on my own.

Fast forward another decade and I have something to show for Nicki's nudge out of the nest. We reduced street homelessness by 87% in Times Square. That project became the catalyst for a national grassroots effort that I led called the 100,000 Homes Campaign. In four years we trained over 150 cities to revolutionize the way they tackle street homelessness This resulted in over 105,000 of the most vulnerable people in America moving off the streets and into places of their own. I co-founded a nonprofit, The Billions Institute, with the aim of solving the world's biggest problems in the next 50 years. I also serve alongside Nicki on the Saroga faculty. I know my overall impact as a leader would have been less had Nicki not woken me up. Rather than trying to figure out someone else's "right answer" she encouraged me to roll up my own sleeves and figure it out for myself.

*Beyond Passion* captures accurately the trajectory of so many nonprofit leaders. We are experts in our chosen field. We are deeply passionate about what we do. We take responsibility for things that make other people curl up in a ball and cry. We do the dirty work and we step into the breach when leadership is required.

Unfortunately, all too many nonprofit leaders operate on "overwhelm." I sometimes notice a deranged pride around how over-worked they are, bragging about late nights and weekends. Gary Snyder said, "We must act as if our hair is on fire and as if we have all the time in the world." Yes, our work is a matter of life or death for billions of people and demands a sense of urgency. And, yes, it is equally important that we take time out for ourselves; to nurture ourselves and to develop ourselves as leaders.

If you are succeeding in your work – and I hope you are – you will get in over your head. It's inevitable. I don't know when it will happen, but you will face a moment of truth just like Isabel does in this book. And when that happens, there is only one question that matters: Are you willing to make the leap from expert to leader? If you are willing to make that leap, this book is your guide. If you aren't, you will burn out.

I don't want you to burn out. I want the best and brightest to stay in this critically important sector. I don't want your impact in the world to be limited by what you can do personally. I want your impact to ripple out through hundreds and thousands of people who are inspired and supported by your leadership. I want you to transcend being an expert and start being a leader.

If you decide that you are willing to take responsibility for developing yourself as a leader, I have some good news for you: I believe that leadership is something you can learn. Just like any craft, learning it takes commitment, dedication, practice and willingness. If you are willing to take the leap, I can think of no better guide for you than Nicki Roth. In this book she distills decades of experience into learnable, do-able skills that you can master: bridging, weaving, detecting, growing and flexing. You bring the passion and this book will help you develop the skills you need to be a more effective leader.

Whether or not you are lucky enough to benefit from Nicki's coaching in person, this book places her wisdom in your hands. It's like she's right behind you, gently nudging you out of the nest, then flying right beside you, pointing out what to pay attention to. Take its lessons to heart and you will experience yourself as a leader in a whole new way.

Becky Kanis Margiotta
Co-Founder, Billions Institute
Los Angeles

# ACKNOWLEDGEMENTS

There would be no book, no Saroga and no dedicated drive to assist nonprofit leaders without my partner in crime, Gavin Fenn-Smith. After a year's worth of discussions about the huge need for leadership services for nonprofits, Gavin leaned across the lunch table and declared, "We should bloody well get serious about this!" We founded Saroga shortly thereafter. This book is the outcome of several years of creativity, resourcefulness, practical application with clients and our collective passion to serve this audience.

It was our great good fortune that Gavin and I were put in contact with Jen Stine: extraordinary thinker, editor, practitioner and teammate. Jen brings skills, insights and her own passion to our endeavors in ways that propel us forward. This book is the culmination of the thinking and work done by the three of us. Even though my name is on the cover, it portrays the Saroga point of view that was developed by myself, Gavin and Jen. I am grateful for their partnership, intelligence and good humor.

On the technical side, I received generous help from Ande Zellman, Charles Denvir, Caroline Berger and Lily Berger. Early readers, Kathleen Yazbak, Muriel Watkins and Becky Kanis Margiotta, provided valuable feedback that helped shape the final version. My heartfelt gratitude goes out to all of you. And a special, very humble, thank you to Becky for writing the foreword.

Isabel's story could not have been told without the countless clients over the years that reached out for guidance. These men and women that are on the front lines everyday trying to solve some of the world's toughest problems are heroic. Theirs is the commitment and passion that changes lives, communities and the environment.

I hope this book will start to change the conversation amongst foundations and nonprofits. The sector needs to focus more primarily on effective leadership and funders need to invest resources for supportive services to these dedicated leaders. Currently there is little discussion, and far less money, being directed into leadership development. Because my clients have proven it over and over again, I can tell you one thing for certain. When development help is given to nonprofit leaders they soak it up like crazy and grow exponentially more effective in their roles. From that position of greater strength, the mission is served better and objectives are achieved beyond expectations.

I am grateful to my partners, colleagues and clients. What I hope for you, dear reader, is that Isabel's story prompts you to ask for or offer up leadership assistance.

# PROLOGUE

How many Executive Directors does it take to change a light bulb? Only one but it will have to wait until after she sends out five notes to major donors, conducts an all-staff meeting, makes a site visit, participates in a community coalition meeting, puts out a few organizational fires, talks with the grant writer and the marketing folks, drafts notes for a board presentation and reviews a report from the program director. Then when she walks into the storage room to find the light bulbs she discovers they are all gone. So she stops at the store on her way home at 8 o'clock that night. With any luck she'll remember to replace it the next morning.

Welcome to the reality of nonprofit leadership. Long days, willingness to do anything and everything, limited resources and laser focus on making a difference.

After years of working with nonprofit leaders and their teams I have observed consistent challenges. Their questions, themes, issues and struggles are predictable. Most leaders become overwhelmed by inadequate infrastructure and processes, limited management capacity of key players, difficult people issues, mission creep (saying yes to everything), contentious partnerships and highly idiosyncratic cultures.

These leaders are smart, dedicated experts in their fields who may or may not have learned how to run an organization before they landed in a nonprofit. For many managing an agency, achieving a mission, nurturing critical partnerships, developing talent and establishing leadership credibility is strictly on-the-job training. Some are able to accomplish incredible things in spite of limited formal leadership education. But the vast majority of nonprofit leaders eventually reach a point when they feel in over their heads. Paradoxically this usually happens when the organization becomes successful and there is a greater demand for services. A smaller and simpler operation was manageable but with growth comes complexity.

This book was written with these remarkable leaders in mind. There are too few resources available to help nonprofit leaders gain insight and learn new skills to drive their organizations to ever-greater success. Most of what is available takes more time and money than most nonprofits can afford. On top of that, good and standard leadership models and approaches don't translate easily to the unique context of these organizations.

Experience has taught me that leadership in nonprofits matters. It matters enormously. But it is rarely discussed or developed. Few connect the dots between achieving their nonprofit's mission and effective leadership. I hope this book changes that. It starts with asking the right questions.

My mission is to help nonprofit leaders, boards and foundations change the conversation. Today the dialogue centers on the mission, impact, scalability and funding. However, there is precious little discussion or investment in effective leadership. My hope is that you will come to realize that leadership is the fundamental engine for achieving your organization's goals.

I invite you into Isabel's world. This is the story of a talented Executive Director, her organization and her team. It could just as easily be about you.

# WELCOME TO AIM HIGH

Aim High was founded seven years ago by an excellent, but frustrated, high school educator. After years of disappointing outcomes for her students, Isabel established Aim High to provide services to underperforming students so they could graduate with their peers. Their programs include a combination of on-site tutorial support, community involvement and family engagement services.

Initial seed money allowed Isabel to hire two colleagues to join in her experiment. Together they were able to persuade one high school in their metropolitan area to pilot two programs. Within the first two years the results were so impressive that more contracts, money and staff followed. By its fourth year, Aim High was scrambling to fulfill all the requests from surrounding schools.

Steady growth and success continued for the next year or so. But in the past 18 months Isabel had noticed some disturbing trends. There were slight dips in the graduation rates at some of the schools Aim High served, funding was slowing down and her staff seemed to have lost steam. She was now sufficiently concerned and ready to take some action.

Isabel knew she would need to involve her leadership team. They comprised:

| | | |
|---|---|---|
| Isabel | Executive Director | Founder (7+ years) |
| Simon | Sr. Director, Programs | 7 years |
| Sandra | Sr. Director, Programs | 7 years |
| Mavis | Sr. Director, Community Liaison | 5 years |
| Chandra | CFO | 3 years |
| Manny | Director, Volunteers | 2 years |
| Fatima | Director, Business Development, PR | 2 years |
| Franklin | Executive Assistant | 4 years |

Although she was unsure about what issues to focus on or what path to take, Isabel was sure of one thing. Aim High was her baby and she needed to take care of it.

# A HELPING HAND

Tuesday was a day like many others. Isabel moved from one situation to the next putting out fires, mending fences and lending an ear. But in the back of her mind was her 1 o'clock meeting with Marshall, the chairman of the board.

Two weeks ago he asked to meet with Isabel. Marshall had taken the reins of the board two years ago during better times and he had been "touching base" more frequently over the past six months. She was so grateful that, unlike so many of her colleagues in the field, she and her board chair had a productive partnership. Isabel knew that she needed to have a more detailed conversation with him.

In fact, Isabel was looking forward to their meeting. She wanted a sounding board, a fresh perspective and guidance about what to do next.

For the past few months Isabel had been aware that something wasn't quite right but she couldn't put her finger on it. To try and sort it out she turned to her faithful friend: the data. What she uncovered was, in spite of their recent efforts and initiatives, Aim High's results in the past 12 months were mixed and lackluster.

The following realities stared her in the face:

- After five years of steadily increasing the high school graduation rates of the at-risk students they served, the last two years showed stagnation;

- Some educational partners were making noise about reducing their financial and programmatic support unless Isabel could kick start further improvements;

- Over the past year Isabel had received complaints from three of their anchor schools about the ineffectiveness of the volunteer staff; and

- In five other schools graduation rates were consistently good and the enthusiasm for the programs remained high.

And these were just the most obvious clues. Isabel also wondered about broader concerns. Was the organization up to speed on all the latest research and methodologies or were they out of step? Did they have the right educational and community partners? Was there enough alignment and commitment to the Aim High goals? Was her team doing enough of the right things to achieve the mission? Was she still clear about what the "right things" were? Did Aim High need to grow? Or shrink? What did the organization need to be to meet students' needs?

But the biggest question looming in Isabel's mind was "What should I be focusing on to pull us out of this slump? What should I be doing differently?"

The past six months had brought a level of doubt that was new to Isabel. When she started Aim High seven years ago she was filled with passion and clarity of purpose. She was convinced that all children, even at-risk adolescents, could graduate high school. After fifteen years in the classroom, a master's degree in the latest teaching methodologies and a grand vision that she was able to sell to a small group of angel investors, Isabel and her team had been determined to alter the lives of urban youths. And they had.

As 1 o'clock approached, Isabel straightened up her desk a bit, took another slug of coffee and gathered her thoughts.

The meeting started with a brief round of hellos and family updates. Then they got down to business. Marshall began on a tentative note. "Isabel, I want you to know how much I respect what you are doing here and that my commitment to Aim High remains firm. But I fear that something is off track these days. I want to hear your thoughts about where things are and where they need to go."

As much as she had prepared for this moment and as comfortable as she was with her relationship to Marshall, Isabel was nervous. "Well, I think it's a mixed bag. Our mission is clear, we've had great success, we've hired some great people and we continue to change the lives of these at-risk students. On the other hand we both know that something is slipping. I've been racking my brain about why this is happening and what to do about it, but my thoughts are all over the map."

"Thanks, Isabel," Marshall said. "I'm hoping that, by the end of this conversation, we can both get some clarity about how to get Aim High unstuck. The board is very optimistic that this hiccup can be worked through. And I want you to know up front that we continue to support your leadership. This is not about replacing you. It's about understanding what is going astray and how to fix it."

Isabel was relieved to hear that she had the board's support. This allowed her to have a very open and productive conversation with Marshall. They concluded the meeting by restating their commitments to each other.

"We have agreed that our results and impact have plateaued and that we don't have enough information to know why that has occurred," said Isabel. "I will engage the senior team in a process to uncover the root causes and possible solutions. You will provide any necessary support including outside experts. We agree that this exploration and solution activity needs to begin immediately and conclude within three months and that we need to see evidence of consistent positive trending within the next six to eight months."

Marshall agreed. Then he added, "In preparation for this meeting, I put together a list of four questions that I would like you and the team to consider. They are based on my combined experiences on the Aim High and other nonprofit boards. The answers we need should emerge from addressing these core issues: increasing our program's impact; establishing sustainable funding sources; strengthening relationships with the board and essential partners; and developing the capacity of the staff and working environment of Aim High."

Isabel expressed gratitude for receiving Marshall's direction and felt his topics were the right ones.

Marshall continued, "Let me add that I was worried this would be a more difficult conversation. I was concerned that you would get defensive and feel personally threatened. Hearing and seeing your enthusiasm to take some new actions just reaffirms the board's belief in you."

Isabel's grin broadened as she responded, "That's so funny! Defensive never crossed my mind. I felt the weight of the world on my shoulders and was looking for guidance and support from the board to get things moving forward again. This conversation was a welcome relief. I needed someone to pull me out of the day-to-day and help me create a plan. Marshall, I can't thank you enough for taking the time to work this through with me. I appreciate your commitment to Aim High and I realize now that I can't remain so isolated. This needs to be a collective effort in order to move forward."

Later that day Isabel had a new thought: I am energized just thinking that I don't have to solve this alone. Her first step was to contact Joseph, a facilitator she had used for several team retreats. Together they designed a series of meetings and processes to get the ball rolling. Even these discussions brought greater focus for Isabel. They debated about whether Joseph or Isabel should be front and center facilitating the team meetings. There were pros and cons on both sides. Ultimately Joseph prodded Isabel to do it herself because he was confident she could pull it off, but also he believed she needed to take full ownership of these exploratory activities.

Although she would have been more comfortable having Joseph facilitate the meetings Isabel realized it was a good idea to stretch herself. She sensed this whole journey was going to force her to think about things in new ways and try new behaviors. She might as well start now. When she shared the plan with Marshall, he was pleased with the design and thrilled that Isabel was going to facilitate it.

# TELLING THE TRUTH

As the team filed into the room late on a Friday afternoon they all assumed the worst. The funding had been cut off. The Board of Education no longer wanted to partner with them. Isabel had cancer. They were all getting fired. Why else would Isabel have called a special meeting at the end of the week? It could only mean one thing: disaster.

When Isabel walked into the room the buzzing and speculation stopped. She didn't look sick. In fact she looked more vibrant than she had in months.

After taking her seat, Isabel said, "I want each of you to think of one word that best describes the current state of affairs here at Aim High. Please share out loud your word."

"Growing."

"Successful."

"Struggling."

"Respected."

"Declining."

"Family."

"Disappointing."

"Hmmm. Interesting, " acknowledged Isabel. "Probably all true. My word is stuck."

Some nodded their heads while others looked panicked. Isabel continued.

"I want us to succeed beyond our wildest imagination. And I believe we can but only if we face reality. We have reams of data that make it clear that the fantastic results we achieved in the first years have flattened or dipped a bit over the past year. We've been trying to fix things but let's be honest: most of the fixes are stopgap measures and not real solutions. We've been trying to rebuild the engine while the car has been running.

"I called this meeting to tell you that we are hitting the pause button and taking time to do a thorough examination of root causes and possible solutions. If we knew what was wrong we would know what to do and we would be doing it already. But I think we are in the dark at this point. Our first order of business is to be honest with each other and talk about what's truly happening. Not just the fact-based truth that is grounded in numbers and analysis, but also our personal truths. The latter is likely to vary among us.

Isabel looked around the table and proceeded.

"I'll start with some facts.

- Seven years ago we opened up shop. It was just Simon, Sandra and myself. Today we have a board with six people, a leadership team of eight, 47 full time staff and nearly 40 volunteers.
- Initially we had one program in one school as our pilot. Today we have three programs in eight schools serving about 500 at-risk students annually.
- In the past five years we have worked with over 2000 students and 1445 of them graduated with their classes.
- We started with just some seed money from some enthusiastic investors and today we have a full time leadership position focusing on funding and PR.
- Today we have critical partnerships with the local school board, churches and community centers.

- We have received statewide attention and are currently in conversations with three other school districts.
- Over the past nine months, in the midst of all this growth, our graduation results have plateaued. Our average graduation rate had been 72% and today it hovers around 70%.
- During these same nine months four key program managers left because they were fed up. The board of education is now threatening to reduce our funding unless we can show improved results within the next six months. We have received 38 complaints from teachers about our volunteers. And the general mood in the office is less energetic and even depressing.

"And now I'll share my personal truth. This work is my passion. That has not changed for me. But as we've grown and become successful, running this place has gotten very complicated. There is so much infrastructure that I spend more time managing things and I've gotten further away from being with the students. That certainly dampens my spirits. I miss being close to the work. My vision was about helping students succeed. I didn't see myself as an executive director. These two roles are not merged in me yet. And I think these divided loyalties is a push-pull that may be hurting us now.

"I suspect that each of you has your own internal dialogue and I would like to hear them. I believe our current results are mixed and if we don't adjust our course appropriately we will start to decline. I want us to get back on track."

The team was speechless. Not because new facts were revealed, no surprises there. They were stunned because Isabel had stated the obvious and made them all face the music. This was met with mixed emotions.

Simon, one of the Senior Program Directors, was the first to speak. "Well, that certainly was a cold splash of water. I must admit that I've been dreading coming into the office for a few months now. Things just feel so all over the place and I spend my days responding to problems. It's taken the joy out of my work."

The CFO, Chandra, chimed in. "I'm so worried about our financial situation but I don't feel like anyone else is concerned. I've been feeling very isolated."

Franklin, Isabel's Executive Assistant, jumped in. "It's not that I don't worry about the issues you've mentioned, but I think our future is bright. Our mission is so bold and our graduates are so inspiring that I still love everything about this job. Including working for you, Isabel."

Sandra, another Senior Program Director, took her turn. "I share some of Simon's sentiments. The job has changed so much in the past four years and I'm not convinced that I'm having a positive impact on the staff, the volunteers or the students. Some days I think we are kidding ourselves because we are not acknowledging that we are off-track. That said, every time one of our graduates signs up for the volunteer training I can hardly contain myself. Here's another fact for us all to keep in mind. Over the past five years 263 graduates have become volunteers and mentors. I guess I'm a bit schizophrenic about where we are these days."

Isabel paused to see if others would speak up. Fatima, Director of Business Development and PR, and Manny, Director of Volunteers, were noticeably withdrawn. Arms crossed and blank expressions signaled to Isabel that this conversation was very uncomfortable for them. She decided not to push.

Finally Mavis, Community Liaison Senior Director, spoke up. "To be honest, right now I feel the first sense of relief I've felt in ages. I can't even describe to you how two-faced I've been feeling lately. I meet with our partners or potential partners and put on my best Aim High face and by the time I get back to my car I am so knotted up because I feel like I'm lying to these people. Isabel, whatever you mean by stepping back to sort this out, count me in!"

# REAFFIRMING THE MISSION

With initial reactions out in the open, Isabel continued. "I appreciate your honesty about how things feel for you. I'm not surprised to hear such variation amongst us. If I fast forward in my mind I hope that we will ultimately arrive at a more uniform experience of things. To start this process I believe we need to recommit to our core."

Isabel stood and walked to the white board and wrote: MISSION. She handed the marker to Simon and said, "Please write what you believe is our core purpose in as few words as possible." Without hesitation Simon took the pen and wrote: "Provide supportive and innovative educational assistance to at-risk high school students so they can graduate with their peers."

"Thank you Simon. Does anyone want to modify this in any way?" Sandra got up and took the marker. In front of Simon's statement Sandra added the words "Our stated purpose is to". And then she added underneath the previous sentence: "But we spend half our time trying to keep the organization running, which we hope will benefit the kids."

Heads nodded all around and voices chimed in with "now that's the truth" and "don't I know it". Isabel was surprised to have struck a chord so early in the conversation and she seized the moment. "It seems we've already hit a nerve. We know what our core mission is but we are spending less and less time in activities that directly touch it. This is what I was trying to share about my experience. So the rest of you feel this way too?"

Simon jumped in. "When I first got here we were much smaller and the administrative duties were manageable. I spent most of my time with teachers and students and I left most days feeling so pumped that we were making a difference in these kids' lives. Now I just feel bogged down with paperwork and personnel issues. That's not what I signed up for."

"I hate to sound like a broken record," began Chandra, "but I keep telling you guys that you don't understand what it takes to run a successful business. I know you don't like thinking of Aim High as a business but that is part of our reality. And if we don't get better at doing that there will not be an Aim High. You think I'm the rigid corporate bean counter who is a pain in your butt when I insist on expense reports and sticking to budgets. As much as I am devoted to our mission, my job is to ensure that we do the right things so we can keep helping these kids."

"You know, Chandra, you just said something we all need to pay attention to," said Manny. "You said we all have to get better at running a business. Other than Chandra, raise your hand if you had any previous management experience before you got here."

No hands shot up but several people offered explanations. Fatima said she hadn't technically been a manager before but she had a great deal of financial responsibilities before Aim High. Simon said he had run some teacher training programs but hadn't been in charge of them. Mavis described two previous positions where she had been a project team leader but she didn't manage the people directly. Finally Isabel said she had been a department head and all of her other leadership roles were more informal.

"I thought I was the only one with limited management experience. Wow, Chandra, now I get why we give you such a hard time. You speak business language and we speak education" said Manny.

Isabel did not want to go down these tributaries just yet. "We've had many conversations about the need to improve our management and leadership skills and we will have many more of these. This is certainly at the root of some of our challenges. But I'd like you to set that aside for a moment so we can get back to our core purpose.

"Here's where I think we are. We have stated that our mission is to provide supportive and innovative educational assistance to at-risk high school students. Does anyone think that is no longer our purpose or that we have lost that focus?" Isabel waited for dissent but heard none. "Does everyone still feel committed to this work?" Again, everyone agreed. "Can we agree that as we go through this discovery process that our mission is front and center? That, whatever new decisions we make, it will not include changing our core purpose?"

Franklin spoke on behalf of the team. "Getting back to our mission would be a huge relief. We have lost sight of why we are all here. If we can keep our focus maybe we can sort things out better."

So far the meeting had exceeded Isabel's expectations. She was aware that there were pent up frustrations and concerns that the team was eager to surface. She knew this would help motivate the members to take this journey she had started. She had to remind herself that she and Joseph had planned well and anticipated a range of emotions. She took a deep breath before moving forward.

# THE ASSIGNMENTS AND A HISTORY LESSON

"Well stated, Franklin," said Isabel. "This has been a great conversation so far and it serves well as the prelude to where I want us to go next. I started this conversation by saying that we needed to hit the pause button and take a deeper look at what might be causing our stagnation. Here is my plan. I want us to spend a day together five weeks from now. And we will all have some significant homework to prepare for that meeting.

"Marshall and I have identified four essential questions that we need to answer. You will work in pairs to address your assigned questions. Over the next several weeks I want you to gather all the intelligence you can on your topic. You can do research, read relevant articles, talk with our students and partners and pick the staff's brains. You are free to approach this in any way you want with this one requirement. Each of you must interview 2-3 nonprofit leaders who may be able to shed some light. We are well connected to a very engaged community and these people have been where we are now. We need their insights.

"Once you have compiled all your data I want you to distill it in two ways. I want you to describe the recurring themes you uncovered as succinctly as possible. And then I want you to select one story you heard from other leaders that you believe all of us need to hear to best sort things out. I don't want any long presentations or 12-page documents. I want the essence. There will be plenty of time for details and analysis once we know what we are dealing with. I want to leave open the possibility that we may be surprised. I don't want us to lock in on anything prematurely. Once you write a huge report you are invested in pursuing that set of ideas. Let's keep our minds open for now.

"At our daylong meeting we will share what we learned and have some time to react. Then I want us to take a week or two to digest the collective wisdom. At that point we will reconvene for a half-day meeting to make some decisions about how to move forward. Does this make sense to you?"

Franklin hesitantly replied, "It sounds like you are asking us to look only at our problems. What about the things that are going well? Shouldn't we be building on our strengths?"

Simon and Mavis raised similar questions. Isabel responded, "I can see why you might conclude that the focus is on the negative but that's why I am being very explicit about keeping an open mind. We might be surprised that there are only a couple things we need to fix and that all the data points to many of the right things being in place. That would be great news. I just don't want to presume anything. We will find out whatever we find out. Then we'll make sense of it. I think I can allay your concerns if I just hand out the questions now."

Isabel pulled out four sheets of paper and handed them out.

- Simon and Sandra: How do we increase the impact of our programs and measure their effectiveness?
- Fatima and Chandra: What funding plan most likely ensures sustainability and growth?

- Mavis and Franklin: How can we enhance our relationships with the board and our external partners?
- Manny and Isabel: How can we increase the growth and capacity of our leadership team, the staff and our culture?

Everyone took a moment to read their assignments. Mavis was the first to react. "Isabel, I'm not seeing a direct connection between the data you shared up front and these questions. How will exploring a funding strategy inform us about why our numbers are slipping? Why aren't we asking the teachers directly what their concerns are with our volunteers?" Everyone else piled on with similar responses.

Luckily Joseph had primed Isabel to expect this confusion, so she was prepared to address it head on. "If I pick up on Franklin's earlier concern about just looking at our problems and then trying to find solutions for them I think we will miss the big picture. Today I've heard you say that you spend too much time fighting fires. Putting a fix on one problem and something new pops up elsewhere. We're all exhausted from this approach. And it's not fundamentally improving anything. We need to step back and see the bigger picture, which is something I fear we did not do seven years ago. Let me remind all of you how Aim High was launched. I know this is familiar to you but please indulge me for a few moments."

Isabel paused before she addressed the team. "After eight years as an English classroom teacher and another four as department head I felt I was missing something because too many of my students were not succeeding. So I took time out to get my master's in the latest learning theories and instructional design. I returned to the classroom to try out all my fancy new ideas and had some success, but not as much as I had hoped. I had a long-held suspicion that what took place inside the classroom was only part of the equation. My studies simply confirmed my thinking. I tried to get my school to institute a variety of mentoring and outreach programs to students and their families. But it had to be on my own time and my own dime. My frustration and dissatisfaction grew. And each semester I felt I was failing these kids.

"The now famous kitchen table moment occurred. I was sitting there with three of my closest colleagues and my husband, who is in banking. The four of them turned to me and basically said they were sick of my bitching and moaning and how many more years was I going to subject myself (and them!) to this misery. My friend Rachel finally said, 'You clearly know what you would rather be doing to help these kids. Why don't you just start your own organization and make it happen?' The rest of the conversation was all over the place but after a while I had to admit that they were all correct. I needed to get out there and do what I believed was right. Okay, decision made.

"It took another eight months to flesh out the idea and put together a very rudimentary organization. My husband introduced me to a few donors who offered the initial funding, my three colleagues volunteered to become the board and I recruited Sandra and Simon as my first employees. I quit my job and we turned my finished basement into our first office.

"Now here is the part of the story that we never addressed directly but I believe is very important and relevant to our present situation. When we began, did we have a mission? Yes. Did we have a strategy? I think Sandra and Simon would agree with me that it was more a plan of action. Did we have a notion, let alone a path, for growth and success? Did we know how to set up record keeping or hiring practices or determine performance standards and metrics? By the time we had five paid employees we were able to get free consulting help to rough out some bare bones infrastructure. But did that mean we knew how to manage an organization? You were hired because you are subject matter experts on community organizing or fundraising or finance or teaching. Assessing you for management or leadership capacity was not a priority.

"So here we are today. In spite of our limitations we have grown and graduated hundreds of students and generated a ton of interest and funding for our work. Clearly we have figured out how to do enough of the right things. But I believe that our standstill in the past 18 months is an indication of hitting a wall. Those limitations are now hurting us. We need to go back and pick up some missed stitches: a strategy, a growth plan and professional management skills.

"What started around a kitchen table and was fueled by our collective commitment to serve these kids is now potentially in trouble. This is the mantra that has been running through my head: Passion is not enough. It worked to launch and sustain us for a while but today it just isn't enough. I hope our passion is always strong but we need something more for our future."

Everyone was still. Manny finally broke the silence. "Isabel, I wasn't around in the beginning but I came to Aim High because of you, your vision, your passion, your track record. I am a believer in your approach because I was in the classroom feeling exactly what you felt. As I look around this table I know my story is not unique. You have inspired all of us to join the cause. I guess I never thought too much about all the issues you are raising now; stuff about strategy and growth and management. To be honest, I just don't know that much about those things and I'm not sure how interested I am in all that. I just want to help these kids succeed. That's why I come here every morning. That said I trusted you enough three years ago to leave my teaching job. If you say we need to examine all these issues now, I'm going to trust you again."

With varying degrees of enthusiasm and skepticism, everyone seconded Manny's opinion. The team left the room with their assignments and blocked off their calendars for their retreat in five weeks.

# THE MORNING RETREAT

It was clear that each manager had taken their assignment seriously and had spent many hours poring over research and conducting interviews. There was lively and thoughtful buzz amongst them and they were all curious what the aggregate information would reveal. Although they struggled, they stuck to Isabel's instructions and prepared to share what they had learned as simply as possible.

The morning of the retreat, as everyone wandered into the meeting room, they noticed several unusual things. For one there were no long tables, just a circle of chairs with a few side tables for drinks. No matter which seat was selected everyone had a bright and gorgeous view of late autumn out of the main window. Sheets of blank flip chart paper were posted on the back walls and all computers and screens were absent. Isabel greeted each person with a breakfast bowl and their favorite morning beverage. She was warm and inviting as she served each manager.

Once everyone was settled in Isabel opened the meeting. "The past five weeks have been fascinating for me. I began this re-examination process because something was off. I knew our numbers were beginning to slip but I couldn't tell you why. I still can't tell you. I was in a slump too. But something happened while I was doing my research. As I gathered more and more information, I noticed all my pistons were firing again and I felt the same excitement I did when we first established Aim High. There was one moment in particular that unlocked my energy.

"I was home fixing dinner after spending most of my day meeting with Mason, the Director of Neighbor-to-Neighbor, and Ariel, the CEO of Mentors Among Us. I was mentally rewinding the tape of those conversations and starting to connect some dots. In my true Isabel-multi-tasking-mode, I wasn't paying too much attention to the simple stir-fry I was preparing for my family. My mind was not in that kitchen so I have no memory of pulling things out of the refrigerator and cupboards. I didn't even notice anything as I put things in serving bowls and called my family to the table: that infamous kitchen table! My husband and daughters remarked on the amazing aroma and variety of colors in the dish. As they took their first bites they pummeled me with questions: Mom, where did you find this recipe? Why haven't you made this before? Did the restaurant give you the recipe? Is this take out? How did you come up with this? At that moment I woke up to my surroundings and stared at this stir-fry I just created. I could not believe my eyes or my palette! It was imaginative, delicious and totally unexpected. In response to all their questions I simply told my family: I was inspired.

"And that is my hope for all of us today. That we will all add different ingredients to the conversation and then take a moment to savor the various flavors and textures. I'm not looking for definitive answers today, just some collective inspiration. Thank you for your participation in this exploration. I don't know about you but I am hungry for some thought food."

## How do we increase the impact of our programs and measure their effectiveness?

Simon kicked off the presentations. "I can't say that I had any 'aha!' moments but I most definitely had much food for thought. Sandra and I explored the question about how we can increase the impact of our programs. Initially we got very hung up on defining impact. I thought we ought to be very precise and find some specific way to measure it beyond how many students graduate. It became clear that I was going down rabbit holes but Sandra was able to save me from myself. We agreed that impact and effectiveness are measured by the number of students that graduate and the quality of life improvements this creates for them."

Sandra picked it up from there. "The programs or services are the centerpiece of any agency. They are the tangible demonstration of the mission. They are what you tell donors about to get them to invest. It's what the ED gives speeches about. It's the reason people want to work for and with you. So programs are number one.

"We noticed very consistent patterns when it comes to increasing the impact of programs:

1. It seems that all disciplines, resources and activities are in service of the programs. Want to make a donation? Pick the program you want to support. Want to determine the budget? Make sure that each program gets what it needs and make cuts elsewhere. Want to expand your impact? Create a new program. Bottom line: the programs rule when it comes to decision-making. They are born out of the mission and are driven by the subject matter experts on staff and the demands for these resources in our communities. Unfortunately, this can lead to a hodgepodge of ever-expanding programs that eventually stretches the organization and staff too thinly. Starting new programs always seems possible. Ending one doesn't happen often enough. The staff is puzzled about how these new programs are decided upon because the process is idiosyncratic and opaque.

2. We found a close link between program design, accountability, metrics and impact. Developing discipline and skills around

rational decision-making and measuring outcomes is a big push these days. This has forced new disciplines on organizations. Funders want to know that their money is making a measurable difference. There are new tools and new skills organizations are being asked to use to make sure that the programs are the right ones and delivering the best results. While this is daunting for most nonprofits, they are slowly integrating this perspective.

3. There seems to be an inflection point where the growth of the organization causes some serious internal challenges. While the grand vision is the ultimate goal, the daily operation still needs to run effectively. A clash emerges where staffs that need to get stuff done get annoyed with new initiatives and programs designed to increase reach and impact. And the visionary leaders get peeved with staffs that now seem risk averse. So this push-pull dynamic surfaces where some want to keep expanding the impact while others are focused on keeping the existing trains running."

Simon continued. "All the stories we heard echoed these themes. The variations had more to do with how each organization faced or did not face these challenges. I will start with an organization that found a clever resolution for some of these issues.

"Coming Home develops existing properties into affordable housing units as a way to solve the problem of homelessness. The founder, Olivia, is inspiring, original, bold and highly effective at bringing together multiple constituents to solve a community's homeless problem. After the first five buildings in Baltimore were completed Olivia wanted to accelerate the expansion. She wanted to move beyond Baltimore, change state and federal policies, address specific high need populations and turn the whole field on its head. But, with each new initiative Olivia introduced, her management team pushed back. They claimed it was beyond their scope, there weren't enough resources and daily operations required all their attention. For a year, Olivia used the board to find new money and push through new activities that the team and staff simply had to make happen. Conflicts and resentments were high.

"Eventually, Olivia was able to understand that there were two separate activities that were core to the organization. One was working in areas around Baltimore to develop housing units and the other was focused on having a significant impact on solving the homeless problem nationally. The local work was focused on daily operations and management. The countrywide work was more of a leadership, social change and teaching function. It was clear that Olivia's passion and talents were best suited for the larger national agenda while other members of her team excelled at managing local operations. The ultimate resolution was creating a new organization with Olivia at the helm that serves as a consultant to communities that want to institute the Coming Home model. So the happy ending was that the visionary founder was free to keep increasing the impact of her model by teaching others and advising policy makers. Most of the original management team was content to keep solving the problem of homelessness in Baltimore while a few members joined Olivia's new efforts."

"We thought this was really creative," Sandra remarked. "The mission remained central and the original operation could remain intact and slowly grow while Olivia went out to conquer the world. Javier's story is completely different.

"Five years ago, Javier was selected as the new ED of Lending Partners, a global micro-financing organization, because he had financial management experience. The board wanted a full accounting of all things numerical. What Javier found when he arrived were outdated and inadequate systems. The board approved a significant investment in a systems upgrade and eventually Javier had good enough data to get a clear picture of where the programs stood. He presented his findings to the board at the start of his second year at Lending Partners. He summarized the key issues this way: 'The good news is that we are solvent and 65% of our recipients are doing extraordinarily well. Their standard of living has improved significantly and about 40% return for a second loan for another venture. The bad news relates to the other 35%. We now know that they have not repaid the loans and their situations have not improved.' The board heard this report as great news. They proclaimed great success and directed Javier to increase lending by 15%. But Javier pushed back.

"He told the board that a 35% failure rate was unacceptable and it was important to understand the problems before increasing the number of loans. He poured over the numbers, reached out to managers, talked directly with recipients, reviewed the financial literacy programs and talked with experts in the field. His board presentation was quite succinct. Javier told them that the difference between those who succeeded and those who failed was connected to the Lending Partners employees. Those staff members who took genuine interest in the recipients, trained them properly, answered all their questions, followed up relentlessly and perceived themselves as coaches tended to have recipients that succeeded. His research indicated that 85% of the cases where someone failed, the services and attention they received from the employee was sub par. The remainder of the failures was due to poor follow through by the recipient. This gave pause to the board and they let Javier do what he thought was best. By using his highest performers as the benchmark, he reassessed and trained all the staff lenders, fired those who didn't measure up and took time for the new standards to be fully implemented. He was still holding off on expanding their programs but expected to begin ramping up in the coming year once a fully competent staff was in place.

"Simon and I thought both of these examples were ones we should learn more about. As Simon mentioned earlier, not exactly an 'aha!' moment but certainly this gives us a lot to chew on."

People started to ask questions but Isabel cut them off. "Simon and Sandra, that was a great way to kick us off. You can see that we are all busting with questions and comments. I'd like to ask the team to record its questions, reactions or comments on the flip charts around the room rather than having a discussion right now. We'll create a thought diary of sorts. When everyone has presented we'll use the notes as the beginning of our discussion."

Everyone found a marker under their seats and wandered up to the separate sheets of paper posted on the back wall. After the team had posted their comments Chandra and Fatima began their presentation.

## What funding plan most likely ensures sustainability and growth?

"Our assignment was to explore plans for sustainable funding," began Fatima. "Initially our research led us to a lot of 'top ten funding tips' articles. There was some overlap between these lists, but not as much as you would think. Honestly, we didn't get to the really good stuff until we began our interviews.

"Synthesizing what the literature seems to say with what we heard happens in real life, we saw these patterns:

1. There are too few funding sources and most organizations are dependent on a small number of big donors. This creates a constant sense of financial insecurity that leads to planning constraints. This scarcity delays decision making on new initiatives, new hires and growth plans; basically anything that requires a long-term commitment. And at moments of significant financial crisis, the boards are often called upon to fill the gap. This is not a sustainable model even though it is the common one.

2. There is a revolving door of business development professionals in most of the organizations that we studied. Many tenures are less than two years. Executive Directors are disappointed with the results and feel the development person over-promised and under-delivered. We didn't uncover the root cause for such high turnover so I just put it out there as a recurring theme. Trust me, this one made me quake in my boots a little. On the other hand it went a long way in explaining why there are always a ton of development jobs posted on idealist.org.

3. Fundraising activities take up an inordinate amount of the Executive Director's time. Estimates ranged from 40-60%. Although EDs know this is part of the job, they believe that a good development officer would manage these responsibilities differently. EDs believe a more reasonable amount of their time spent on fundraising would be closer to 30%.

4. There is a current of entrepreneurial, opportunistic, enthusiastic and aspirational fervor that plays a role in decision-making.

Excitement and possibility rather than objectivity and mission focus cause agencies to say yes to certain funding or growth targets. Organizations that stay within the scope of their missions and identify their priorities and capabilities do better at sustainability. Growth is calculated on human and financial capacity."

"We were a bit disappointed that we did not discover the Holy Grail about funding," said Chandra. "We did see ourselves reflected in some of these trends but we were still trying to crack the code on sustainability. We talked with both EDs and development folks and, as you can imagine, heard very different perspectives. So we selected two organizations that found different paths to financial security.

"Clean Water Advocacy, a 25-year-old organization, was deeply in debt and the board was analyzing whether or not to close up shop. Ultimately they decided to give it one last chance. They replaced the Executive Director and were lucky to hire Li who had deep experience in the field and had previous management roles. Beyond his resume, what impressed the board the most were Li's infectious personality and his re-imagination of CWA's core mission.

"Li described the first two years as grueling. He knew what kind of financial situation he was walking into but he didn't realize how difficult it would be to engage the staff. He assumed, falsely, that they would join him in the fight for survival. Instead he was met with resistance, hostility and even several legal complaints. Over the course of 18 months Li made a series of difficult decisions; people were let go, new people were hired, programs were eliminated and new partnerships were formed. He brought in a new development officer who he hoped would get them on track financially. Sadly, this did not occur. It was Li who ultimately came up with the solution. After one of his many public presentations the head of an environmental think tank approached him. Long story short, CWA was invited to be the clean water arm of the organization complete with adequate funding and infrastructure resources. CWA would remain independent with its own board while providing all the clean water research and services.

"In the two years since the new structure, things were going very well. CWA was solvent, the board was thrilled, the industry was excited by the new work and they all lived happily ever after. But I don't want to lose the major point to this story. To quote the board chair directly, 'None of this would have happened without Li. We were failing by doing the usual good practices. But Li had a bold new vision and the charisma to sell us on his ideas. We had interviewed a lot of people but when he walked into the room we knew there was something unique here. And what we felt was exactly what the think tank President felt and what every donor feels. People open their wallets for CWA because of Li.' This organization found a unique partnership that provided a much better shot at sustainability. We should be so lucky!"

"You can say that again!" chimed in Fatima. "On a different thought path related to funding and sustainability I spoke with Juanita, the founder of Honor and Dignity. Her story was more about scope creep and not managing the money and programs effectively. As Sandra mentioned, this example is something we need to pay attention to.

"Honor and Dignity, headquartered in Washington D.C., was established after the first Gulf War in the 90s and offers support services for veterans. What started as mental health services has expanded to include job training and placement and a client-run soup kitchen. Juanita, the founder, is a veteran herself and has a special way of relating to the clients. When I asked her to describe how the funding and programs at Honor and Dignity were expanded she summed it up this way. 'We had a history of tacking on all sorts of programs that seemed to be the right idea at the time so eventually even the vets were confused about what we provided. The board finally took me to task by insisting that I evaluate the effectiveness of each program and return to them with a more coherent and focused plan.' Juanita's military training was very useful for what followed.

"She assessed the financial viability and actual impact of each program and concluded that three core programs were highly valuable and the other four were draining limited resources. In short order she shut down those services and redistributed the funds. Then she introduced the staff to quality control tools. That did not go over well. Juanita was accused of asserting tough military disciplines on a social service agency but she persevered. She hired a Quality Control director who could implement and oversee new processes.

"Once the programs had been cleaned up and were measurably effective she presented a longer-term plan to the board complete with detailed financial statements. She proposed two pilot programs to augment the core services that would be contingent upon long term funding. The board appreciated how modest the plan was and committed to exploring new revenue sources. Juanita wanted us to understand that 'more is not necessarily better but that better is certainly better.' She warned us to keep our programs focused and to put rigorous tools in place to constantly monitor cost and impact."

The team took ten minutes to stretch and write their remarks on the charts. Isabel noticed the muted murmurs. She picked up a mix of thoughtfulness and numbness. Even she was vacillating between feeling stimulated and overwhelmed. She had no idea where all this information was headed.

## How can we enhance our relationships with the board and our external partners?

Mavis took the floor. "Franklin and I researched what we need to do to enhance our relationships to the board and our partners. We're actually going to present these separately because there are different things to learn. Let me start with the partnerships and then Franklin will address the board issues.

"Not unlike Fatima, I got a bit nervous about what I learned in this process. It can all be summed up this way: making partnerships work is very challenging and critical to success. This wasn't news but it was a dose of reality.

"These are the common trends for organizations:

1. The unequivocal truth is that partnerships are a critical success factor for nonprofits. Organizations that did not build strong ties either failed or had limited impact. These relationships are

pipelines for resources and door openers to constituents and multipliers for creating real change.

2. In spite of the importance of these partnerships the stories and results are very mixed. There is positive intention from all parties but navigating the dynamics is challenging. Aligning agendas and approaches, developing productive relationships and meetings, and sorting out the hierarchy between and within each organization were common issues. The biggest pain was managing the competition for limited resources. Partners all try to cooperate and share but in the end the slices of pie are very small.

3. There are a surprising number of broken and troubled partnerships. About half of the articles and stories were about extreme conflict, passive aggressive and disrespectful behaviors. In situations with this level of dysfunction the organizations were experiencing degrees of negative publicity, withdrawal of funding, staff departures and choppy effectiveness.

"I want to share an especially complicated but enlightening story about partnership relationships. Marge was hired as the new Executive Director of Our Families two years ago. The board had long believed that the previous leader was problematic but they dragged their heels to make changes until they had created their new strategy. So when Marge arrived her task was to take over a struggling organization that was in danger of being shut down, implement the new strategy and make loads of changes. Among her many priorities, fixing and elevating the community partnerships were front and center.

"She went on a two-month listening tour to each key alliance to explain the new strategy and clarify how the partnerships could work together going forward. She was flabbergasted and disheartened with what she learned. The feedback she received about her staff boiled down to three major issues. Our Families managers and staff behaved as if they were king of the heap and insisted that their methodologies were not open to discussion. On top of that the clinical expertise they claimed to have was, in fact, sub par. And last, the partners were engaged in passive aggressive behaviors to freeze out their Our Families peers. No one wanted to work with the agency. The only silver lining to all this bad news was that these partners saw Marge's arrival as a good sign. Everyone was willing to give her a chance to improve the situation.

"Then Marge turned her attention to her own staff. She went through a series of rational and objective activities with the staff that began with making her expectations about these partnerships very clear to all. She got a lot of pushback from the staff. She worked with the management team to redesign the liaison roles and then use performance management tools to assess the current staff for fit with the new requirements. People were moved, developed or exited, including supervisors who did not support the new protocol. It was a lot of heavy lifting over 16 months but the proof was in the pudding. Marge continued to seek out feedback from the partners over the course of the changes and there was a noticeable shift in productivity and collaboration about 10 months in. When we talked Marge was pleased with the progress but felt it was important for her to stay involved at the highest level until she was fully confident that the new relationships were consistently maintained. Her greatest evidence of the turnaround was the board now held up her office as the example to all others. They were now the top performer and Marge spent time coaching her peers about how to transform their partnerships.

"Franklin and I agreed that our team needed to hear what Marge was able to accomplish. Rather than focusing her energy on berating her uncooperative partners she took a hard look at her own staff. She fixed what she had control over. Trust me, this already has my wheels turning about some things I need to do differently."

Franklin got the team's attention with his first words. "You will be hard pressed to find a nonprofit board that is truly effective. My research and interviews are filled with stories of mediocrity. Coincidentally, the same is true in the corporate world. It seems that getting the right people on the board doing the right things is just challenging. Of course the nonprofit boards exist within a unique context.

"These are the usual dynamics:
1. The membership of many nonprofit boards comes from the founder's personal and professional circle. 50-75% of

the team is close-in associates who support the vision and passion with their time and money. They focus on gathering financial resources, some strategy work and being as hands-on as the Executive Director needs them to be. They are usually benevolent and dedicated people who want to be part of making the dream a reality.

2.  However, these friendly connections do not necessarily lead to productivity. Issues arise when a board is not involved enough or is too involved. Or a board can be too removed to be knowledgeable about daily operations and issues. Sometimes a board is just a group of people that talk a lot but don't get much done or lack focus and alignment around priorities. Many sources reported serious conflict between the ED and the board chairperson. In other words, just because your friends are serving on the board that does not make it certain that they will be effective and helpful.

3.  The skill set of each board member is a new part of the discussion. In the past, the major criteria for board membership were prominence in the field or community and money (both your own and in your network). In the past 5-10 years there has been a push for more professional expertise: strategy, marketing, communication, accounting, human resources. While nonprofits are pressured for greater accountability, performance metrics and hardcore evidence of the impact of their work, boards are being asked to play a more active and technically savvy role.

"I got the sense that the conversation about board effectiveness is very much a work in progress. Some nonprofits are moving towards member selection based on critical skills but most boards and organizations are right in the middle of this transition.

"One organization that is on the other side of this is the Association of African American Professionals (AAAP). It is an all-volunteer professional society that has chapters across the United States. I spoke with Marcus, the director of the Atlanta chapter. AAAP has been around since the 60s and started as a small network of advanced degree African Americans in New York City. The mission has changed very little since the beginning: to provide a community for professional learning across many disciplines. With exponential national growth in the past decade the headquarters had to re-examine the role, structure and effectiveness of the chapter boards. When Marcus came into the ED role a large group of volunteers who had day jobs ran the chapter while a board of 25 people had uneven oversight.

"Four years into his tenure, Marcus began a series of in-depth discussions with the AAAP national President suggesting that an unpaid director and an over-stuffed board were no longer effective. It wasn't rational to ask a full time professional to also run a large organization for free and expect great results. As for the board, many people stayed on indefinitely because of the prestige it offered rather than any value they brought to the organization. The upshot of these talks was that Marcus became the first paid Director of the Atlanta AAAP chapter and was given free rein to make significant changes. He redefined the role of the board and then carefully selected a hands-on board chair who would have majority responsibility for board meetings and engagement. Together they chose eight people who could perform in this new environment. Only three people were existing board members; the rest were new people.

"This transformation has yielded some impressive results. The Atlanta chapter now has 879 members, a dozen new corporate sponsors, a new college outreach program and is routinely cited in the local newspapers. Marcus believes that having a paid director was the first critical move but that moving away from the legacy board positions was even more important. He had to ruffle some feathers but it was worth it for the overall health and growth of the organization. The role clarity, new skills and new structure have created an effective board. What started as a pilot program is now the model for all the chapters. Nearly half of them have made the same transition.

"My biggest takeaway from this story was that it's important to hit the refresh button when it comes to long-term practices. Mavis and I don't think that the Aim High partnerships or board are in immediate danger but this exercise helps give us a heads up."

This was exactly the kind of learning Isabel was hoping for. "Me too! I feel like we are getting a chance to address some things ahead of the really bad stuff that could happen. Thanks to both of you for putting all that together so clearly. Let's take a moment to record our thoughts and have a 15 minute break."

The team was subdued as they wandered to and from the restrooms. "I feel overwhelmed by all the information." "My mind is jumping all over the place." "I'm so glad we aren't experiencing some of the problems that have been presented." "I'm relieved to know that what is happening here is typical." "I haven't a clue where all this is leading."

## How can we increase the growth and capacity of our leadership team, the staff and our culture?

Isabel turned the meeting over to Manny to present their findings. "This question turned out to be much broader than we imagined. We found ourselves researching talent development options, leadership criteria, agency structure and organizational culture. So we tried to zoom in by identifying the priorities for Aim High. Staff and leadership development and culture emerged as our biggest concerns. Isabel and I agreed that we were taken aback by what we uncovered and hope that we all head these issues off at the pass!

"These are the headlines:

1. We found several white papers that sounded the alarm about the high demand for nonprofit leaders and the limited supply of people who are well prepared to step in. On the ground in these organizations the staffs are shouting for professional development and promotion opportunities. Unfortunately most nonprofits are ill-equipped to meet these needs. They don't have budgets for staff development or internal learning programs or even enough different seats to move people into. This leads to either high turnover or staff frustration.

2. Because we have such a large volunteer staff we explored that as well. Unfortunately the news about volunteers is not great. Article after article said that managing volunteers is like

herding cats. Each person is eager to provide important services to a cause. They are passionate and committed. But when it comes to following the training guidelines things fall apart. They all have their own ideas about what works best and are not shy about doing their own thing. This creates tremendous inconsistency in the quality of the services. When the managers try to bring this under control, they discover that they have no rewards or consequences to hand out for performance. Even when volunteers are taken to task, managers have a hard time 'firing' them because they are so devoted to the mission.

3. The management capabilities in nonprofits are limited. As it is with the staff, there are few programs or resources to help managers and leaders grow and become more effective. This seems to lead to a host of issues: lower results, poor supervision of staff, quirky management practices and difficult cultures.

4. The vast majority of nonprofits are intentional about defining missions, values and desired work atmospheres. These are communicated regularly and used as part of formal performance evaluations. If someone acts out of line feedback often takes the form of 'that is outside of our values'. In some cases (more than we imagined!) there is a serious disconnect between the values and staff behaviors. This was especially true in organizations that weathered difficult changes in leadership or direction or staffing requirements. A negative and vocal subgroup forms that is resistant to change, hostile to new leaders and generally a disruptive force in the culture. These situations create enormous leadership challenges. The goal is to bring the behaviors and work environment back to the core values."

"Without much commentary at this point," continued Isabel, "Manny and I agree that Aim High really needs to pay attention to these trends. We believe we are already experiencing some of these concerns. So we selected two stories that offered the best insights for Aim High.

"A visionary and charismatic leader named Rajiv founded the Great Harvest Food Bank in 1988. His dream was to work with farmers, grocers and restaurants to gather up unused food that was still fresh enough to serve to those in need. The combination of his charm and the vast community need caused Great Harvest to grow rapidly. One of its cornerstones was the ethos of a collective: a non-hierarchical structure, team-based and values-driven. Between 1997 and 2009 there were many ups and downs and loads of changes. Rajiv left the organization under a cloud for undisclosed reasons, three different people tried and failed as ED, half the locations were shut down and there was closer scrutiny by the government of the bookkeeping. Amazingly, while all this was happening, the essence of Great Harvest continued, many of the original staff stayed on and the place was still solvent.

"In 2009 the board promoted Miriam, the operations manager, to become the next executive director. During her first year she uncovered layer after layer of dysfunction. Although Rajiv had been gone for 10 years, he was very much alive in the culture. The staff members who had been there at the beginning revered him and whispered multiple versions about why he actually left – all of them putting him in a good light. Newer staff were invited into this clique and indoctrinated into 'the way things really work around here'. The disconnect between the stated norms and the staff behavior was wide. Miriam did her best to go back to the original values and use those as the guideposts for behavioral expectations. She provided frequent feedback to individuals who stepped out of line and tried to get the staff focused on serving the greater good rather than any personal agenda. She told me that she made very little progress on the culture but was able to make some good business decisions. Then there was a watershed moment. A particularly negative staff member went off on a vile rant in a staff meeting for all to see. Something shifted in Miriam at that moment and she firmly told the person to leave the building and never return. She then turned to the staff and invited all others who leaned in that direction (even if it was more polite) to leave as well. Two more people left. She dismissed the rest of the staff and told them to reconvene in 30 minutes. During that time Miriam called the board chair and the lawyer and made sure that everyone was informed. They agreed to handle the details of the dismissals for her and supported what she was about to do next.

"It was clear that the remaining staff was stunned when they reentered the meeting room. Without anger or threats Miriam told the group that she had been remiss in not putting an end to the harmful behavior sooner but that everyone must expect that will not be the case any longer. The stated values were to be taken seriously. If people behaved in contrary ways, they could expect to be warned once and then exited from the organization if it happened a second time. No exceptions. That happened about three years ago. Miriam learned that day that if the leader keeps looking the other way when the values are violated, no one could be expected to take them seriously. And when these dynamics are left unattended, real damage happens to the staff, to the organization and to the people who are served. It took about a year and a half for the environment to improve. Miriam became a more effective leader, nearly all of the old guard left and the return to living the values allowed for multiple points of view with interesting solutions. So, very hard work but a good outcome in the end."

"Miriam's experience is my worst nightmare," said Manny. "I hope we never get to that place and I'm worried that we are all sitting here with a sense of dread. So please indulge me a few more minutes so I can share what I learned from another organization about staff development. I think this will help us avoid the long-term deterioration that Miriam faced. Can you all listen a little more?"

"Oh geez! Please don't leave us shell shocked over that story. Give me hope!" Sandra blurted out.

So Manny proceeded.

"1-2-1 is a national mentoring program that matches 10-18 year olds with adults to provide guidance and support in completing school and venturing into the world of work or college. They've got chapters in most major metropolitan areas and have a great track record. Most locations have a paid staff of about 60 people who manage the operations and oversee 200-600 volunteer mentors. I was able to speak with Liam, the long-term Los Angeles Executive Director. In particular I wanted to hear how he deals with having a mostly volunteer work force. The national 1-2-1 headquarters struggled with a litany of complaints in the 90s, most having to do with a lack of commitment from the mentors who seemed to disappear after making an initial connection with the student. This infuriated the parents. Very long and messy story short, 1-2-1 instituted a quality control process complete with checklists. Once the LA office was trained on the new tools they saw things turn around. Today their success rate (based on number of matches, longevity and job or college placement) is 78%. Liam hopes to improve that.

"That got us into the topic of staff development for the paid employees. Because it is such a strong national brand, new college graduates bang down the door to be one of the paid staff. The good news is that he gets bright people who are devoted to 1-2-1. The challenge is that they want to keep growing professionally and expand their scope of responsibility. They want to take on management roles and introduce innovative programs. I laughed when Liam described this because it's a pretty great problem to have. The problem is that, with such a small paid staff and a flat organization, there are few opportunities for these people to develop. The average tenure of 75% of the staff is 2-3 years. Liam sees 1-2-1 as the first career stop for many young people and then they move on to places with more opportunities. As much as possible he creates learning moments at the agency. Outside speakers come once a month, there is an internal mentoring process and he sets aside some money for folks to attend conferences. He tries to support learning and growth even if there are limited ways to apply that at 1-2-1. When he attends national 1-2-1 meetings all the EDs describe the same dilemma. For now they have concluded that the highest priority is serving the needs of the students. This means that high staff turnover is a given and that hiring is a constant.

"I think we can learn a lot from 1-2-1 as we sort out what to do with a volunteer work force and paid staff development needs."

"Thanks for that respite Manny," Isabel said. "Everyone take a moment to chart your final thoughts then take a quick stretch. Lunch will be here in a few minutes and then we will spend the rest of the day trying to digest what we learned today."

The afternoon discussions were interesting yet inconclusive. The team shared their reactions to the charted remarks, the crazy stories and the key themes. There was laughter and lively dialogue but mostly there were more questions. Isabel thanked the team and promised to synthesize all the information and present a plan within the next two weeks.

# PRIVATE REFLECTION

What a day! Isabel felt drenched with information and tangled in the voices of her team. She was so grateful to finally be alone with her own thoughts and emotions. She desperately needed some privacy to sort things out. She pulled a chair up to the picture window and stared out at the autumn trees.

Her mind went in twenty directions at one time and she was flooded with contradictory emotions. She was nervous and excited. She was hyper-stimulated and drained. She was hopeful and doubtful. After fifteen minutes of this buzzing she got herself a cup of tea and reviewed the team's comments on the flip charts plastered around the room.

As she reread the lists Isabel was struck by the vast number of remarks that were about leadership or about discussions the management team needed to have. That mirrored her recurring thoughts throughout the presentations in the morning. She heard so many stories about solutions being traced back to the leader:

- We have to get back to the basics of what made our programs and approach great. We've become distracted
- I need to learn more about managing and growing my team
- I'm worried that I won't have a job at the end of this process
- I like the CWA think tank story. We may need to find our own big partner
- I would like us to get to a point where money isn't such a constant focus

- Do we want to increase our impact or the number of students served?
- The ED is the starting point in building the community ties
- Partnerships are complicated and require a level of maturity and savvy. I'm not sure we are always meeting that standard
- There is a double bind for the ED: she has the passion/message but fundraising can't be her only priority

- I wish we took more time to explore the board issues. I think we are not using ours well enough
- So what skill sets do we need at this point on our board?
- Our current tracking and monitoring of our programs isn't enough
- I wonder if we trust our staff and volunteers too much. We are assuming they are doing the right things but maybe they aren't

- Are we assessing our volunteers properly or just taking anybody? We need a stronger screening and training process.
- I know our staff is frustrated because we don't have any growth opportunities for them. Should we just plan for turnover or find a way to fix this?
- We should discuss the possibility of moving away from a volunteer model

decisions about growth, high impact connections, thoughtful analysis of various issues, assessment of talent on the management team and staff. Okay, that was one glaring observation.

Next, Isabel realized there was only one team consensus and that was that everyone was feeling overwhelmed. Her team was split between two courses of action: exploring tactics and innovations to

- Are we being too polite with each other? Maybe this team is part of the decline
- We need to create a strategy to guide growth rather than grow and then figure out what our strategy has become
- We are using funding as the primary deciding point. It needs to be more than that
- There are a lot of negative rumblings amongst the volunteers but we haven't dealt with this head on

- Our culture has become very low energy. Maybe we need to have some different types of conversations with the staff
- We may have to accept some things that we don't like. Stuff like continuous staff turnover or money constraints
- As I listened to the Our Families story I realize I don't have what it takes to do what Marge did

get the graduation rates on the upswing again and investigating further a bigger picture view of exactly why things were stalling.

Then Isabel thought about each person on the team.

Simon surprised her the most. She got whiplash listening to his two completely opposing points of view. On the one hand he wanted to get further into the weeds and do more research on critical success factors for achieving impact. And then he did an about face, citing the literature and suggesting this was all about leadership effectiveness. After all these years, she was used to Simon's thought process but he seemed especially conflicted today.

As always, Mavis and Sandra were able to see the macro issues. Isabel saw this every day in how they approached the work; the students could only succeed if the relevant, larger issues were addressed. She chuckled when she recalled how Sandra pounced on Chandra for always bringing up the financial concerns. It's a good thing Chandra can hold her own, but Isabel had to side with Sandra on this one. Sandra challenged the team when she said, "We can't let our financial worries be the end-all and be-all for making decisions at this point. Is anyone here going to feel great about our work if we keep operating but our students aren't succeeding as we expect them to?"

Although Chandra can be singularly focused on the numbers, she is very good at what she does. Isabel would hate to lose her so she was willing to tolerate Chandra's inability to think about the organization as a whole. Chandra could get very testy and frustrated with the team but, as long as everyone can ultimately work together, Isabel wasn't too concerned. "But if I'm worried about losing her maybe I need to know more about what is going on for Chandra," was Isabel's next thought.

And then there was dear Franklin: the eternal optimist. His outlook was just right for his administrative role but if he ever aspired to be more than her right hand he would need to get comfortable with disagreements and making tough calls. Today's meeting was a good reminder that she needed to help Franklin develop as a professional.

It pained Isabel to watch Fatima in the meeting. She didn't see anything new but Fatima's discomfort and silence just reinforced Isabel's growing assessment that things were not working out. While everyone else was able to focus on what will be best for Aim High, Fatima couldn't stop talking about the difficulties of her role and her worries about her own future. She set herself up as a significant outlier today and made it easy for all to see her as a weak link. Isabel made a mental note that, apart from whatever path the organization takes, she had to face the situation with Fatima head on.

Manny. Isabel pondered this one. He seemed to be in over his head: not a strong manager, not enough systems or processes in place, not enough supervision of the volunteers. That said, his passion for the students, his innovative teaching ideas and his eagerness to learn worked in his favor. At many moments during the day he was unabashedly honest about his lack of management experience and his willingness to learn. Isabel wasn't sure what she needed to do with Manny yet.

Thinking about each team member, Isabel recognized that not everyone was going to be able to take whatever the next steps were going to be. So that was the second big takeaway from the retreat: Isabel needed to evaluate the readiness of each team member to step up their game and change people out who were falling short.

Finally Isabel asked herself some tough questions. "Am I being an effective leader for where Aim High is today? Do I have all the skills I need? Can I trace all the problems of the past year back to my doorstep?" She didn't have clear answers to any of these questions. But she was certain that she needed to do something different if Aim High was going to be a sustainable successful organization.

As she stared out the window, Isabel found herself thinking about the kitchen table moment and asked herself if there had been much thought given to how she would lead an organization. She remembered vague references to being a boss but the whole focus was on defining the mission and figuring out how to get things up and running as quickly as possible. In fact, she only recalled a handful of conversations over the past seven years about her leadership. She saw herself as a teacher and an innovator, not a leader. Well, it was time to expand her self-definition and take a serious look at her leadership.

Isabel realized that leadership was something she simply hadn't learned much about yet. No classes, few role models, limited experience. This wasn't about capability. Thinking of this moment as a learning opportunity was a good fit with her identity as an educator. She imagined she could get comfortable with that.

Putting these reflections together started to excite Isabel. If the root cause of Aim High's current challenges has more to do with leadership and management she needed to have all the right players on her team and she needed to step up her own leadership game. As she gathered up her stuff to leave she wondered, "How does one learn about leadership? What does that even mean?" Without a pause she answered, "I don't know yet but I want to find out." She packed up her bags and knew she would be sending emails to some trusted colleagues to get some ideas.

# REACHING OUT FOR HELP

Isabel's network of nonprofit peers and corporate friends offered up several referrals for consultants who focused on leadership development and organizational effectiveness (two new vocabulary words for Isabel). She had phone conversations with five consultants who all sounded quite smart and reputable. They each described a range of training, coaching and consulting services that might meet Isabel's needs. It was hard to distinguish one from another and no one quite struck a chord with her--until she spoke with Talia.

The conversation began with Talia inviting Isabel to tell her how Aim High began and what was happening now that required attention. "Tell me your story."

When Isabel had finished Talia asked a simple question. "What do you think you need to do to move things forward?"

Isabel laughed out loud. "I asked myself the same question. And I couldn't answer it specifically. I think I don't know what I

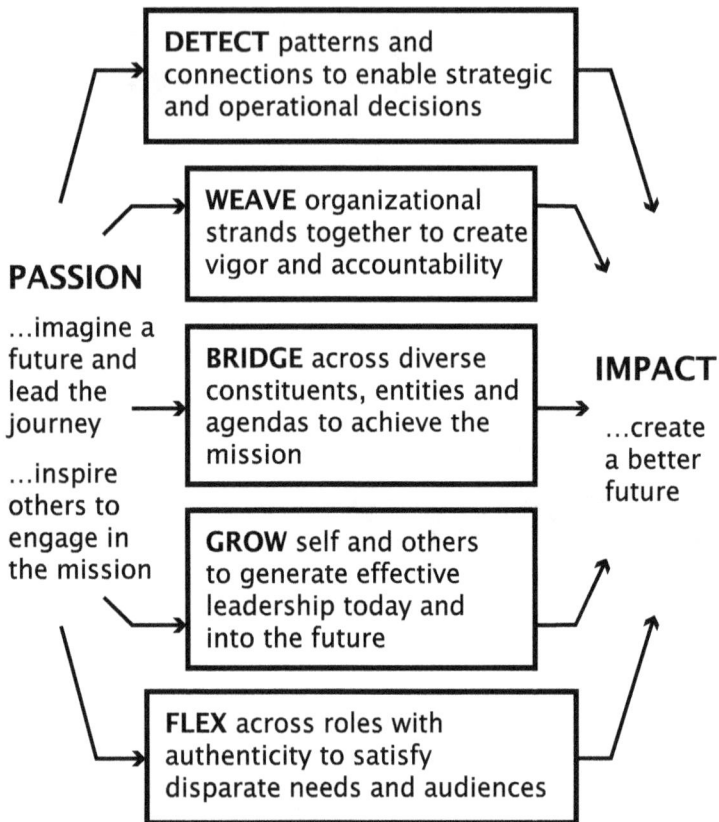

don't know. I just believe that I am not doing enough or enough of the right things."

"Clearly you have been effective on many fronts," Talia said. "You have strengths that have gotten you this far. Now the situation may be calling for some additional skills that are less developed. If you would like, we could set up a meeting that will help you to clarify exactly what you need to do next."

Isabel found it easy to talk with Talia and set up a face-to-face meeting for later in the week. "Is there anything I should be thinking about to prepare for our conversation?"

Talia reassured Isabel that there was no homework required. They would just talk things through until it made sense to Isabel. But she did ask Isabel to send her notes from the retreat so she had more background information and context.

## Making sense of the situation

Talia and Isabel sat at the small round table in Isabel's office. Once they were settled in, Talia began the conversation.

"Thank you for sending over the summary notes from the retreat. I must say that your team did an incredible job picking up on all the hot issues that nonprofits face routinely. And the stories were so rich. I hope that you will be able to see the big picture by the time we finish our discussion."

"That would be a relief. I'm still swimming in all that information," offered Isabel.

"Let's just dive in then," continued Talia. "I'd like to walk you through a leadership model that is specific to nonprofits. It will help frame your strengths and gaps and provide some insight about how to address the challenges for Aim High."

Talia began, "At the very core is Passion. Much like your story, most nonprofits are established because someone has a vision of how things could improve for a particular population or issue if only certain services and partnerships were created. The founder is passionate about a situation and she is able to inspire others to join the cause. When you go back to many founders' kitchen table moments, they often have the 'why not me?' revelation. Why continue complaining about something and hoping that someone will come along to fix it when you can be the fixer? So passion is the genesis of the organization and persists as the raison d'être. It infuses the culture and forms the basis for many hiring decisions. Very few people join a nonprofit just to have a job; it's a calling for most."

Isabel let Talia know how much she agreed with this. "Honestly, on the bad days it is my belief in these students that keeps me going. The whole reason I'm willing to do whatever it takes at this point is because of my passion and commitment."

Talia continued, "It is fundamental. One thing it seems you don't consider in your self-perception is that your vision and approach to your work has prompted others to participate. That's leadership, by the way. If no one bought your view of a better future then you wouldn't have an organization. So don't sell yourself short on that dimension. That said passion is not enough to sustain an organization.

"Let me explain this in reverse. If you look at this diagram you see Passion at the front end and Impact at the back end. Impact is what nonprofits hope to achieve – usually some kind of improved future for a group of people or a change in policy or a better planet. Corporations seek different outcomes: profits, products or services. Except for a few fields, Impact is not featured as a desired outcome of the company's work. So if the starting point is Passion and the end result is Impact what has to take place to get from point A to B? Make sense so far?"

"Very much so," responded Isabel. "I never framed things quite like this but every time my husband and I talk about the differences between our work we always get to a point where we just declare that it's two separate universes. So what is all this stuff in the middle?"

Talia explained, "I believe there are five abilities that nonprofit leaders need to demonstrate to be successful. This first one is Detect. This means that the leader needs to look at all the moving parts, such as the staff, the operations, the programs, the strategy, the external partners, the environment where the work is conducted and then be able to connect all the dots. She needs to see the inter-connectedness and how things function together. This requires seeing around corners to anticipate changes, noticing patterns and constantly innovating and responding to shifting needs. This is not all that different than what a corporate leader needs to do except the context couldn't be more different. In the nonprofit world, leaders are basically trying to create change and their constituents and partners come from multiple points of view. A skilled leader understands the needs of each group and how they can work in concert. These leaders also know how to engage the staff, set priorities and make operational decisions so that all these disparate parties align around the mission."

"Okay, that makes sense," said Isabel. "You're saying that I need to be a big picture thinker. I need to be someone who can put all the macro pieces together in ways that lead to success for the organization. And if we define success as a 90% graduation rate for all our students, I need to make sure that we have all the right parts and they are working together."

"That's right," Talia nodded. "Then going from that broad perspective you need to make sure that your organization is plugged in and operating to support that view. The model identifies that as Weave. What are the daily operational activities that you have established for Aim High?"

Isabel thought for a moment. "We do lots of tracking: money in, money out, number of students, how they are progressing, how many graduates, parent and teacher communications. We have some rudimentary hiring guidelines and staff salary and benefits oversight. We have a leadership team that manages the programs and the people. My team would tell you we do too much fire-fighting which I'm coming to understand means that we don't have enough operational practices in place."

Talia picked up where Isabel left off. "You and every other growing organization I work with. When you are only 15 people you don't need much in terms of disciplined work processes but once you have grown to 40 or more nothing runs very smoothly when things remain so informal. There is so much time eaten up by just taking care of the basics to keep the trains running. If there isn't a standard way and timing of submitting monthly reports, for instance, then you can't get your hands on reliable information to let you know if things are moving in the right direction. You also don't get a clear picture of how the staff is performing. Without some uniform procedures and standards it is tough to hold people accountable or measure how well they are achieving the Aim High goals. Weaving together all these threads of people and management processes and creating simple and effective practices makes life easier for everyone.

"Here's the caveat about Weave," Talia continued. "If a leader doesn't take care of the internal workings of the organization then she will inadvertently create an environment that can become quite dysfunctional. I'm guessing that you spend more time than you care to on conflicts between staff members." Isabel nodded reluctantly. "One thing I know for sure about human beings in group settings is that if there are few protocols in place weird dynamics will emerge. Some will look benign, like withdrawal or passivity, and others will feel more negative, like aggressively seizing control or establishing unproductive cliques. I know you could tell me stories about some of the families you serve and I'll bet the ones that have more structure and firm expectations have a higher probability of their students graduating."

"I never made that connection before," offered Isabel. "That is so insightful. I could give you three dissertations on how structure, discipline, high expectations and persistent monitoring enable at-risk adolescents to stay in school and excel. Without those guardrails or touchstones, they will look for groups outside their families or schools that can provide that. I think you saw in our retreat notes that some of the stories we heard were quite messy when it came to people and work environment issues. Our team was so relieved that we are not in that boat. But it seems to me now that all these people issues that are distracting us are signs of the beginning of trouble. If we don't get on top of this right now then things could sour for us too."

Talia could almost hear the gears turning in Isabel's head. It was a relief to talk with a leader before things deteriorated. Talia continued. "I agree completely. Just to be clear, both Detect and Weave are insights and actions that for-profit leaders manage too. The difference for you in a nonprofit is the complexity of your context. You are one part of an entire community of people and organizations that care about at-risk students. Each of you has your own approach and financial resources and boards. As a leader in this mixture, you have to facilitate collaboration and alignment rather than competition. So for Aim High to achieve its goals you have to interact with many people that you have no direct control over. That brings me to Bridge.

"I think of Bridge as uber-interpersonal skills. As a leader you need to be able to connect with donors, staff, community leaders, government officials, students, teachers, parents, key influencers in your field and the guy that holds the lease on your office space. That's a tall order. You need to read your audience, adjust your style, establish trust and credibility and nurture meaningful long-term relationships with such a wide range of people. This is where there is a huge distinction between you and a corporate CEO. In all my years I never heard of a corporate CEO being pressed to have crazy great interpersonal skills. It's a nice-to-have but not critical for getting results. For you, Aim High can't achieve its goals without building those bridges to critical partners."

"I remember the day that I realized the importance of relationships," Isabel remarked. "I had one of those weeks where I was racing from one meeting to another; the board, my leadership team, the neighborhood coalition, individual staff members, teachers and so on. I was talking with the principal at one of the schools we serve. She was venting about one of the teachers. When she took a breath I told her that it sounded like she didn't trust this teacher. Her response was to tell me that she could always count on me to do more than listen, that I can hear the message that is being delivered. She went on to say that feeling deeply heard allowed her to trust and respect me. I had been taking these skills for granted up to that point, even though it was evident to me that tons of people don't do what I do. I know this is one of my strengths as a leader and advocate. I also know that 80% of every day I am required to interact with others so I'm glad this one comes more naturally to me."

Talia smiled. "That's a great story. And you are fortunate that you are good at relationship building. I'm certain that is why you have been able to accomplish so much in a short period of time. As we continue to sort out what you need to do next it's likely we'll circle back to these strengths as part of a game plan for getting Aim High unstuck.

"Let me ask you a question about your staff. Do you have much turnover?"

Isabel had just been looking at this data recently so she was able to answer quickly. "In the first five years, we were hiring at a steady pace but in the past two years we have had about 10% of the staff voluntarily leave. For a small organization, that feels huge."

Talia replied, "Actually 10% is about average. But you are right, in a small agency that creates disruption. Do you know why people left?"

"There were several who left because of life events; a baby, moving, going back to school. But the recent departures of four program managers was particularly troubling. I spoke with each one and tried to persuade them to stay. They were all bright, talented and very effective with the students. There were two major reasons they all gave: lack of professional growth opportunities and frustration with not being able to generate positive momentum in the organization. This is when I knew we were in trouble. These are very different issues and I feel an urgency to solve both of them."

Talia let Isabel's comments hang in the air for a moment before she spoke. "It sounds like you have just identified one catalyst for change. Four talented people hit a wall organizationally and professionally and they didn't see a more satisfying future. Loyalty to you or the cause will only keep great people around for so long. They need to be nurtured so they can develop as well as be engaged in the problem solving. Referring to the model this leadership requirement is called Grow.

"Let me address the professional growth issue first. Most nonprofits are small with limited managerial roles so there is no traditional movement up a ladder. The next option is to provide challenging assignments that expose a staff person to new ideas and skills. There, too, there are few choices. Most nonprofits seek out subject matter experts that are hired for their depth of knowledge and moving people around into new roles or project teams is not so easy to do. What about training or more classroom type professional development? Well, that takes money and time and actually isn't very effective for adult learners. Mentoring and coaching run up against the same time and financial constraints. So what options does a small nonprofit actually have for developing the staff? Of course, I can offer lots of guidance about how to do this with limited resources but the best solution is to make learning a routine organizational commitment. I'm guessing that, as a group of educators, this could be solved rather easily."

"Ha! Don't we just fit the cobbler's shoeless children to a tee. That issue would actually be fun to fix. I would love to spend time engaging the staff in learning experiences." Isabel's energy visibly shifted. She was smiling, her shoulders relaxed and she was on the edge of her seat.

Talia continued. "This organizational wall your former program folks raised is actually why you and I are sitting here today. Something is stalled. The graduation rates are not increasing, there are complaints from some of your partners and there is not yet a plan of action to get things moving forward. They were just the first ones to wave the red flag.

"Here's where I want to connect some dots for you. Imagine that a year ago you noticed a few troubling patterns emerging. You were hearing more frustration from the staff, you were seeing the numbers on certain programs taking a dip and there were more articles in the paper about poverty in the primary neighborhood you serve. At the same time you noticed that you were spending more and more time just trying to keep the place operating. Then imagine that you pulled your team and others into a room and presented data related to these trends. You asked the program managers to dig into the slipping numbers and come back to you with a clear picture of what is happening. You asked your community liaison person to talk about what she is hearing from other organizations about the impact of more severe poverty in the neighborhood. Then you encouraged her to host a meeting of all the community players to discuss possible responses. And then you met with staff members in small groups to learn more about their frustrations. And you were thinking about adding a part time administrative person. Where do you think you would be today if those things were on your radar a year ago?"

Isabel's mood shifted again. This time she seemed more still and pensive. "I don't know the answer to your question. I'm not sure we would have created forward motion if we had addressed all those things. I'm not sure the managers would have stayed. But I do think that we would be facing the challenges as a group. We would be having the right conversations and working hard to figure things out. We would not be avoiding issues and hoping that things would magically turn around. In fairness, I did ring the bell on the decline in program success but we never came to a good understanding or any solutions. Are you suggesting that I dropped the ball?"

"Not in any way," jumped in Talia. "What I'm trying to point out is that if Detect and Weave were among your strengths then you would know how to address the staff frustrations and stagnation. It's not an issue of focus or timing. It's an issue of your leadership development. You have identified that you are great at Bridge and I'd guess that none of your partnerships are in trouble. And you mentioned that you and others are adept at Grow but just haven't made it a priority. But you didn't say much about Detect and Weave. Those are high order big picture and operational skills that you probably haven't learned yet. You didn't do anything wrong. You simply need to learn some new things."

Isabel took a moment to let this soak in. "I know that as a teacher I should readily embrace what you have said but I'm struggling a bit. Aim High is my baby and I feel totally responsible for everything. I acknowledge that we are at a tough spot right now and I feel that is my fault. My inner voice is negative but you are telling me I didn't do anything wrong."

"Try this. Think of one of the students you have helped. Think of someone who had great potential and was willing to put in the time but he had missed out on some fundamentals earlier in his schooling. So he was struggling in spite of his best efforts. Did you even have the thought that he was doing something wrong or that it was his fault?" Isabel shook her head. "And when he turned to you in utter exasperation did you tell him that he simply needed to learn some new things and that you would help?" A nod. "And when that remarkable moment occurred when it all came together for him and he began to make significant progress did you remind him that he had the capability to learn anything he set his mind to? That there was nothing wrong with him as long as he was open to learning?"

Isabel got the point. "Okay, okay. I get it. Funny how we grown ups think we should already know everything. I suppose it's just as tough for us as it is for an adolescent to reveal that we don't know the answer to something. I clearly need to start taking some of my own good advice!"

"I'd love to see that," Talia agreed. "Let me just tell you about this last leadership element, Flex. Again, this one you won't find on any job description for a corporate CEO but it is the story of your life. Nonprofit leaders wear a crazy number of hats in any given day or week. You can move from inspirational speaker to advisor to advocate to manager to facilitator to mediator to grant editor to coffee maker to donor wooer. You need to shift gears constantly, adjust to your audience, take on tasks large and small and do all this with authenticity. What I mean by authenticity in this context is that no matter whom you are interacting with you need to be consistent, sincere and true to yourself. You can't have one face for the office staff and another for a wealthy donor. So shifting gears does not mean changing masks. How do you think you do on this dimension?"

Isabel laughed. "I've got this one nailed! My friends get dizzy just listening to me describe a typical day. I even keep a couple changes of clothes in my office because I never know what will come up on any given day. But I assume all leaders are good at this one."

Talia responded. "Many people who choose nonprofit leadership roles know this is part of the job and that suits them just fine. But not all of us human beings are wired to bounce from one thing to another especially when the task and the people can be so dramatically different. Flex is a culture shock for many corporate folks who enter the nonprofit world. They are used to wearing only a few hats.

So that's the model. Let me ask you if this is a helpful way of thinking about your leadership and what is happening in your organization right now."

Isabel gathered her thoughts first. "My first reaction is most definitely. For one, this framework resonates with my reality. I appreciate being able to see where my strengths are and what I still need to learn. I can even see how my interpersonal skills will come in handy when I dive into Weave. In terms of the current organizational issues, it seems that my growth in a couple areas would go a long way in creating a more productive environment. But I don't see a clear connection between my improved leadership and all the issues we are trying to solve."

Talia said, "I don't expect that to be obvious at this point. We've done a mini-Isabel assessment in this conversation and uncovered what is working well. The next step would be sifting through your data and retreat notes and determining what the patterns are and what are the 2-3 most critical issues to tackle first. Then it is using those real problems as your learning lab to try new leadership behaviors. Ultimately, it is the marriage of sharp problem identification and new leadership actions that will get Aim High out of this slump. And if all that goes well then you have an expanded set of abilities that will help you to work through an endless number of organizational challenges.

"Let me make one additional point here. Today we focused on you. But I want to be clear that there will be learning and growth for your team as well. You can't get the organization moving forward alone. Part of your journey will also include assessing and coaching your team to try some new actions. I want to be realistic with you about this. As you become more clear and confident in some new skills, you will look at your team through a different lens. You will bring to the front of your mind some nagging thoughts you've been pushing to the back. Is this one performing up to your expectations? Is that one helping or hindering the change? Does that one have the right skills? Can that one learn how to be a more effective manager? This is a natural part of this development process and you will find it challenging. But there is tremendous learning that takes place as you shape and build your team. Even if some of the moments are difficult it is a huge win for Aim High, the students and the team."

"I wondered when you would get around to my team," Isabel said. "What you are saying confirms what I've been thinking. One of my insights from our retreat is that I admire and respect every member of my team, but I'm not sure they are all up to the task. For the time being, I insisted that they not worry about their own futures. But I think the unspoken truth is that not everyone will be suited for the changes and growth that need to occur. I feel such split loyalty about this. On the one hand, these people have helped us to succeed, but on the other hand, they may not be the right people to help Aim High get to the next level of success. This one will be tough for me," sighed Isabel.

"And that's why I like to raise the issue early," said Talia. "I want clients to know what they are getting into. Let me summarize where this conversation has left us. Walking through the leadership model has highlighted your areas of great strength and where you need to learn or enhance other skills. The model even shed a bit of light on what organizational and people issues might be at the root of the stand still. I recommend that you take some time to reflect on this discussion, talk with some other consultants or trusted advisors and then decide what path forward makes sense for you. How does that sound?"

"Great," replied Isabel. "You have given me much to chew on and I need some quiet time to see what I think. Just so you know, I need to move quickly. The board wants a game plan yesterday and I have a meeting with my team at the end of next week to propose a course of action. Not to mention that I want to get started immediately. There are pressing issues about funding and expansion breathing down my back that I need to move on. In an ideal world I would feel things shift into gear within the next eight weeks. Are those crazy expectations?"

Talia stifled a chuckle. "Crazy? Maybe. Doable? In my experience, when a leader is highly motivated and ready to try some new things you can see some movement quickly. If we move forward, our first order of business is to develop the plan that becomes the map for the journey. It is built around your current challenges and factors in the context, priorities and timing of your needs."

Isabel and Talia thanked each other for a productive meeting. Isabel promised to get back to Talia within the week.

# A PLAN IS HATCHED

For the first time in months the fog was clearing for Isabel. Between the information gathered by the team, conversations with three different consultants and some valued guidance from Marshall she had a good sense of what needed to happen next. The first order of business was to call Talia to let her know that she wanted to engage her help. They sat down for their planning meeting just days after their initial encounter.

Isabel began the conversation. "Thank you for making yourself available on such short notice. I really want to get started immediately. I want to leave this meeting with a plan for moving forward that I can take to the board and my team." Talia let her know this was possible.

"Let me begin with how I have put the puzzle pieces together since our last conversation. The leadership model helped me frame my thought process. I found myself thinking about the early years, where we are now and where we need to be going forward. Here's a diagram I made while I was sorting all this.

---

**Core from the beginning**

# PASSION          IMPACT

---

**My natural strengths**

# BRIDGE          FLEX

---

**Untapped strength**

# GROW

---

**Skills I need to develop**

# DETECT          WEAVE

---

"When I think about the beginning of Aim High, my Passion was a burning flame that drove everything. And it was clear from our mission statement that our Impact was very well defined. So I knew what was driving us and how we would measure success. I think those have been constants throughout these seven years. The only thing that has changed is wanting to, no pun intended, aim higher with our graduation rates. So I am clear about the front and back end of the leadership model.

"Where it gets interesting is all this stuff in the middle. As a new organization, I focused most of my attention on Bridge and Flex. I was forming relationships all over the place: donors, school officials, community partners, teachers, the Board of Education. My attention was on building the bridges Aim High needed to launch and achieve early success. Not coincidentally that meant that Flex was my modus operandi. Honestly, when I think back it is all a blur. In the midst of all that activity I was able to hire the first fifteen people (including several of the folks on my leadership team), define our holistic approach, get contracts to start four programs and see the first students graduate. The board was basically a group of my friends or former colleagues and I mostly turned to them to help raise money or make connections. We were mutually hands off during those years.

"From an organizational perspective, I would say the early years had very little to do with Detect, Weave or Grow. I was fortunate to bring on some like-minded and dedicated people who managed to make things work well enough. We didn't have adequate office space, we had very few staff meetings and we didn't even see each other that much. They were all out in the field working with the students, teachers and families. Eventually, I created a few key roles on my team so they could take over some of the stuff I was doing: community liaison, fundraising, program development.

"Then we hit a major growth spurt about four years after we opened for business. Our dramatic success with the students we served became well known in the area. The requests for services nearly tripled and we were completely understaffed to handle that. This was the moment when I began to work more closely with the board. If we were going to say 'yes' to everyone, then we needed to staff up. So, we moved our office, hired nineteen educators and moved to a model of using trained volunteers. I brought on two business savvy board members, hired a CFO and a volunteer manager. We started having weekly team meetings and monthly staff sessions. We built internal processes only when it became necessary. In many ways I was attending to the tasks you call Weave. I wish I could tell you that I was doing more than being reactive and flying by the seat of my pants. We were just building on our success and trying to reach as many students as possible. I think some of what was built is held together with rubber bands and paper clips. I'm so lucky to have staff that is willing to put up with it.

"What I am coming to understand is that lots of things started to slip out of control during this time of growth. From our conversation, I now see that I don't know enough about Weave or Detect: two capabilities that could have built a more solid operation. Disgruntled staff, complaints about volunteers, disappointing results and inadequate standardized operations all began appearing about two years ago. I have been responding by fire fighting, working harder and putting on a brave face. Clearly not the best path.

"Now we have plateaued and are at risk of losing funding. The most troubling thing for me is that people are now wondering if our success was a fluke that can't be sustained. That is eating me up and that's why I have such a sense of urgency. To put it simply, Aim High has to reassert its credibility. I now see that my limitations as a leader and how we operate are at the root of our problems."

Isabel finally paused. Talia was impressed but not surprised. "Your analysis is fantastic and it sounds like you have a sense that you need to grow, rather than that you did something wrong. I'm glad you let go of the guilt. Let's see if we can refine your thinking even further. You've presented a lot of data on what is slipping or stalling. Your team did a lot of research to see if you could uncover some themes. And now you have identified two aspects of leadership that need your attention. All of that covers too much ground. You've talked about your sense of urgency so let's start there. If you could solve two issues in the near term, what would they be?"

Without hesitation Isabel blurted out, "Get the graduation numbers moving up again and get our house in order. Each of those is huge and there is probably good information in our notes to point us in the right direction. I'm more confident thinking about the programmatic solutions than I am about the organizational ones. But that makes sense. One plays to my strengths and the other is a challenge."

"Right," said Talia. "So let's agree that increased graduation rates and organizational effectiveness are the two big goals. Those will still need to be broken down into smaller targets. For instance, when you say getting your house in order are you thinking about retaining key talent or standardized processes or strategic decision making or staff development?"

"All of the above," said Isabel.

"Can you identify the one thing you could improve in the organization that would have the biggest impact on the Aim High objectives?"

Isabel pondered that question for a moment. She replied, "I'd have to say having the right staff with the right skills. We need to get to all of it, but if we don't have the best people providing the services then our results will surely drop and then we won't have an organization."

"I agree with you," continued Talia. "Here's the thing. In the past six months you've become more aware there are problems. Then you did some broad research internally and externally and that was like drinking from the fire hose. Somewhere in the process your sense of urgency kicked into high gear and now you want to attack all of it. What I can tell you about adult learning and organizational growth is that it works best when you pick one or two high impact issues and take a series of bite-sized steps to change your actions. We are just not wired to change too much at one time and if you tried to do that it would backfire. So our plan for moving forward has to be first things first. Once you experience forward momentum then you can add one or two more new actions. For change to stick it has to become integrated into your daily habits."

"Okay, so you're telling me that I have to focus my attention," affirmed Isabel. "I can do that. Let's spend the rest of our time today, then, creating a plan that I can share with the team and the board that has the greatest chance of near term success."

# TEAM MEETING DEBRIEF

What happened in the team meeting confirmed many of Isabel's current thoughts. She was anxious to run them by Talia.

Isabel began, "I know you prepared me for the range of reactions to the change plan but I must admit that I left the meeting deflated. They seemed more enthusiastic at our retreat and digging into research and new input. But when it came down to here's-what-we-are-going-to-do most of them gave me serious attitude."

Talia smiled and said, "I know that you and your organization are extraordinary Isabel but the team's reaction was ever so normal. I tried to warn you. When change is a thought exercise it can be very stimulating but, when it gets down to a real plan that requires real actions, most of us regular human beings will balk. I always think of it as the 'when I said we needed to make changes I didn't mean me I meant you' syndrome. So what happened?"

"The beginning actually went very well," Isabel explained. "I took your suggestion and thanked them all for their efforts over all the years, and more recently, for joining forces to sort things out. It turns out, you were right that I don't praise them enough. They all noticed the new behavior and urged me to make a habit of it. I was having an inner dialogue with you while they were giving me the feedback – telling you that some Grow actions can be very small steps indeed!

"Then I described that the overarching goal was to increase the graduation rates and that we were going to focus on talent development and operational efficiencies to get us there. Everyone was confused about how I arrived at this conclusion so I explained it and they generally understood how I was connecting the dots. For a moment, everyone seemed to buy it and then it fell apart.

"Chandra did her usual gloom and doom about funding. Mavis thought we should focus on our partnerships. Sandra and Simon wondered why we weren't doing a deep dive into program effectiveness. Manny was terrified I was directly criticizing him and leaving him out of the loop entirely. And I could hardly contain myself with all of Fatima's worries about her own position. The conversation got so intense that poor Franklin all but curled up into a little ball."

Talia interrupted. "So how did you deal with their reactions?"

"At first I just sat back and let them respond in the moment," continued Isabel. "But that voice in my head was a bit freaked out. We don't usually have such heated exchanges and I wasn't sure what would be best. Then I remembered our discussion about my interpersonal strengths and thought about what I would do in a tense meeting with some of our partners. So I told them that I understood each one had a different point of view and that their first reactions might change once they have a chance to think things through later. In fact, I encouraged them to take some private time to do just that. But for this meeting, I wanted to give them the outline of the plan.

"Then I made it clear that I was the person who needed to change and learn the most and that I had engaged your help. When I put the focus on me they began to simmer down a bit. I told them a bit about what you and I had discussed about my strengths and areas for new learning.

"Just as you predicted, in the next minute they were asking if they needed to do a parallel development process. I was so glad we rehearsed this in advance! I told them that I had to make some changes first but they should anticipate and welcome new growth for themselves.

"I noticed that most of them eventually came around and some of the emotions had settled down. I think you'll like where I left them. I ended the meeting with a story I'd like to share with you.

"There was a master teacher whose advice was sought out by many parents. He was revered as experienced and wise and it was well known that his guidance worked on even the toughest problems. One day a frantic mother approached the master and sobbed, 'Oh great teacher, you must help my son. I can't get him to stop eating sugar. All day long all he wants is sweets and nothing I have tried works. His health is suffering, he doesn't sleep and he is falling behind in school. Please tell me what to do to make him stop.' The master told the mother to go away and come back in 3 months. Terribly upset, the mother left with her son.

"Three months later she returned to implore the teacher again. 'Oh great teacher, the situation is getting worse. My son hardly eats anything except sugary treats. Please, you must tell me what to do to make him stop.' Again the master sent her away and told her to return in one month.

"After a month the mother returned with the same, but now more urgent, request. Through her tears she said, 'I fear my son is so sick with sugar that he will suffer a terrible fate. Please, great teacher, what must I do to help him?' Again she is sent away and told to return in one week.

"The mother returned to master the next week and asked the same question as before. 'Oh great teacher, what do I need to do to get my son to stop eating so much sugar?' To her surprise the master responded with this instruction, 'Tell him to stop.'

"The mother was so stunned that, after she caught her breath, she begged the teacher to tell her why he could not have told her this the first time they met. His reply was simple. 'Because first I had to stop eating sugar myself.'

"I told the team that they will participate in new ideas and new habits and new learning. But first, I need to master a few tricks so that I can lead the way."

# THE JOURNEY BEGINS

With Talia's help, Isabel embarked on a plan to develop additional leadership skills. Using the current situation as her learning lab, Isabel focused her attention on three critical areas: staff evaluation and development, volunteer assessment and training and an integrated reporting system. She took lessons from several stories from the team retreat and reached out to some of those leaders. Javier, from Lending Partners, and Liam, from 1-2-1, were especially generous with their insights and sent their guidelines and tools so Isabel did not have to invent her own wheel. She pulled Sandra and Manny into the process and they jointly created an aggressive plan. She was more stumped by the systems issue and leaned on Chandra to explore possible solutions. Marshall also had some leads in this area. The goal was to find low cost off-the-shelf software that worked for smaller organizations.

In their private discussions, Talia gave Isabel the chance to express her doubts and frustrations as she experimented with new behaviors. Isabel came to realize that she wasn't in touch enough with the day-to-day activities and that she was making too many assumptions that things were running smoothly. The more time she spent with Sandra, the more she realized there was great variation in the quality of the staff. How had that happened? This provided the opportunity for Isabel to clarify her expectations for hiring criteria and performance monitoring with Sandra. Because of their long-term relationship, this was uncomfortable at first but eventually they discovered renewed enthusiasm and greater synchronicity.

Her conversations with Manny about the volunteer program were more challenging. Talia helped her understand that she had not set Manny up to succeed. There were no standards or guidelines in place when he arrived. Isabel simply told him to meet with the churches and community centers that offered to partner with Aim High and then trusted him to make it work. There was no clear assessment that these were the right partners, no application process, no evaluation of the volunteers' performance and very limited training. Talia, Isabel and Manny agreed they needed to rethink the entire notion of using volunteers. As they dove into this several things became clear to Isabel. For one, being opportunistic (using a ready made group of volunteers) required much more thought before jumping in. This highlighted Isabel's need to learn more about Weave and Detect. Secondly, she had to create the conditions for staff to succeed. Manny had voiced his struggles regularly but she had not responded adequately. She came to realize that the program managers that left had similar concerns. She wanted Manny to stay at Aim High so she left open all possibilities, including a different role that would suit his skills better.

Five weeks into the change plan Isabel was feeling optimistic. She was seeing more of the big picture and how all the pieces fit together. She tried many new behaviors with varying results and she was aware of a shift in her overall leadership style. She stated clear expectations more frequently, set tighter deadlines, praised staff regularly and said "no" more often. She felt more focused and energized and she saw small signs that the staff picked up on that. There were more smiles, less complaining and more new ideas bubbling up.

Isabel wasn't sure exactly how Aim High would be transformed through this process but she was quite certain of two things. The graduation rates would slowly increase and she would become a more effective leader. She took Marshall out for a nice dinner to thank him for giving her the kick in the pants to get things moving forward.

# EPILOGUE: DO TRY THIS AT HOME

Nonprofits are complex, intense and idiosyncratic. That is good news and bad news. The good news is that remarkable people come to contribute to the mission and get amazing things done. The bad news is that without effective leadership and some sane organizational habits all those good people and great outcomes are not sustainable. If you believe that you and your organization are hitting a wall or are in trouble try these first steps.

Take an honest assessment of your leadership strengths – and gaps. All organizations are a reflection of the leader so you want to be certain that you are putting all your best abilities forward. If you experience gaps in the organization or staff, that may have as much to do with you as others. Find a trusted advisor for a heart to heart. Select someone who is used to providing you with honest feedback. Identify the strengths that are helping the organization and areas where you need to learn some new skills. The nonprofit leadership model presented here provides a positive, strengths-based framework for your self-assessment.

Identify the 1-3 greatest pain points for the organization. What issues are hindering your progress right now? Your team will give you a long list but you need to focus on the critical few that are preventing you from achieving the mission. Is it about the talent in your organization or creating more productive partnerships or saying "yes" too often or avoiding addressing staff problems? Determine which one or two concerns are having the greatest negative impact on fulfilling the mission.

Create a leadership development plan for yourself that will have the biggest impact on resolving the pain. It may be that some of your strengths are currently being underutilized and need to be brought to the forefront. You may discover that you have avoided addressing the critical issues because you are less skilled in those areas. Develop an aggressive learning plan that will allow you to experiment with new behaviors that will result in solving your current and pressing concerns.

Find the best learning resources you can afford. Seek support from your board and funders. Ask them to make an investment in your growth. Look for resources that are geared specifically towards nonprofits. You may need a consulting group or an individual coach. Ask your nonprofit peers where they have gone for developmental help.

Make a deep commitment to grow and change. This work is very personal. It requires that you admit that there are things you don't know how to do. Experiment with new behaviors that feel awkward and then practice until you get it right. The journey will not always feel good but eventually you will be delighted with your growth. And nothing creates more change than success. And that's when the fun kicks in.